GOD LIVES IN GLASS
Reflections of God through the Eyes of Children

Robert J. Landy, Ph.D.

Foreword by Sandy Eisenberg Sasso, author of *God's Paintbrush*

Walking Together, Finding the Way

SKYLIGHT PATHS PUBLISHING
WOODSTOCK, VERMONT

God Lives in Glass: Reflections of God through the Eyes of Children
© 2001 by Robert J. Landy

For information regarding permission to reprint material from this book, please mail or fax your request in writing to SkyLight Paths Publishing, Permissions Department, at the address / fax number listed below.

Library of Congress Cataloging-in-Publication Data
Landy, Robert J.
God lives in glass : reflections of God through the eyes of children / Robert J. Landy ; foreword by Sandy Eisenberg Sasso.
    p.   cm.
ISBN 1-893361-30-6
1. Image of God. 2. Children—Religious life. I. Title.
BL205 .L35 2001
291.2'11—dc21   2001001932

10 9 8 7 6 5 4 3 2 1

Manufactured in Malaysia

SkyLight Paths, "Walking Together, Finding the Way" and colophon are trademarks of LongHill Partners, Inc., registered in the U.S. Patent and Trademark Office.

Walking Together, Finding the Way
Published by SkyLight Paths Publishing
A Division of LongHill Partners, Inc.
Sunset Farm Offices, Route 4, P.O. Box 237
Woodstock, VT 05091
Tel: (802) 457-4000   Fax: (802) 457-4004
www.skylightpaths.com

For Mackey and Georgie.

Foreword

by Sandy Eisenberg Sasso

IN THE FOLLOWING PAGES YOU WILL BE PRIVILEGED TO ENTER THE IMAGINATIVE WORLD OF CHILDREN AND HEAR what they have to say about God. Some of what you read will make you laugh, some will make you nod with approval. Some selections will make you sad and others will make you wonder what it is that you think about God.

Too often we assume that there is only one way of talking about God. We call God by names that we have been taught are acceptable and forget that we can call God from our place, out of our own particular experience. Our children can help us remember.

Once, during a service at my congregation, I was teaching a group of children about the many names we use for God in prayer. We talked about how, in many of our prayers, people call God *Father, King, Lord, Eternal One*. But I suggested to the children that we could call God by other names as well. Sometimes we might call God *Mother, Healer, Friend, Maker of Peace*. After the lesson, I asked the children to tell me what their favorite name for God was. Most of the youngsters said *Mother* or *Friend*. A young boy, whose mother had been suffering from cancer for most of her son's life, raised his hand. When I recognized him, he said, "I would like to call God *Healer*."

The imaginings of children about God are an invitation to us to engage ourselves in a conversation about life's ultimate questions. This little book shows that, in many ways, we and our children are partners on the sacred journey.

So often we believe that what is most necessary in this holy pilgrimage is finding the answer to what or where or when is God, but our children can teach us that more important than the answers are the questions. Our sacred journey is less about finding and more about seeking. Children are not afraid of seeking, of questions without answers.

Rabbi Menahem Mendl of Kotzk once asked his disciples if they could tell him where God dwelled. Surprised, they answered, "How can you ask such a thing? Is not the whole world filled with God's glory!" Then the Rabbi answered, "God dwells wherever we let God in."

God Lives in Glass is a window that allows us to glimpse at the places where children let God into their lives. If we can allow ourselves to see through their looking glass, we might just find those places and moments where we can let God into ours.

SANDY EISENBERG SASSO is the author of many award-winning books for children, including *In God's Name, God's Paintbrush*, and *God Said Amen*. She is the second woman ever to be ordained a rabbi (1974) and the first rabbi to become a mother. She is active in the interfaith community and has written and lectured on the renewal of spirituality and the discovery of religious imagination in children and adults of all faith traditions.

Acknowledgments

I BEGIN BY THANKING THE INSPIRATIONS AND GUIDES FOR THIS PROJECT—MY CHILDREN, MACKEY AND GEORGIE. My wife, Katherine, has been with me throughout the birthing of this project, providing a word, a nudge, a tear whenever necessary. I am grateful for her eye and ear and heart. I also wish to thank Sue Emmy Jennings for her inspiration. Her childlike spirit shines through these pages. I was very fortunate to have found superb and collaborative editors, Sandra Korinchak and Martha McKinney, who carefully shaped and kneaded this project along with their colleagues at SkyLight Paths.

There were many helpers from all around the world who unselfishly devoted their time and prodigious skills to sit with children and explore the mysteries of the spirit. I am indebted to the following: Lawrence Arturo, Ann Ball, Judith Bernard, Nuno Barreto, Nic Billy, Carole Bramlett, Melanie Bramlett, Asra Chapnick, Chiao-hua Cheng, Jim Cosgrove, Mafalda Costa, Avivit Deby, Vincent Dopulos, Ciara Douglas, Daphna Eyal, Ali Goughti, Roger Grainger, Annamaria Grimaldi, Avi Hadari, Craig Haen, Grainne Hall, Matilde Hall, Uwe Hermann, Clive Holmwood, Rina Itzhaki, Urmila Jain, Jaben Kahn, Stanley Kalathara, Young-Ah Kang, Martha Kemp, Jinsook Kim, Line Kossolapow, Veronika Krumnow, Linda Lampitt, Sara Lavner, Mary Lou Lauricella, Kory Lorimer, Darko Lukic, Barry Lynch, Nellie McCaslin, Roisin McKeever, Uma Singh Mahajan, Torben Marner, Alistair Martin-Smith, Shevy Rahat Medzini, James Mirrione, Hiroko Muraki, Junko Muraki, Emily Nash, Galila Oren, Gioia Ottaviani, Marcella Palazzolo, Nadine Permutt, Donna Ray, Mrs. A. C. Rhinehart, Delfim Ribeiro, Antonella Ristagno, Katerina Robertson, Graciela Rojas-Bermudez, Aliki Romano, Manuel Rosado, Veronica Santoyo, Edith Shawyer, Ciara Stuart, Joyce Sykes, Anat Tanamy, Elektra Tselikas-Portmann, Janice Valdez, Milan Valenta, Rachel Worthington, Stanislava Zaprianova, Noga Kaplan Zvi, Pastor Paul Chamberlain and the parents and children at Calvary Church, Kingswinford, West Midlands, Britain.

Most of all, I acknowledge all the children who participated so openly in this project. Their wisdom and grace are ladders that I never tire of climbing.

Introduction

As long as I can remember I have had a burning need to make sense of the universe and my place in it. When I was young and frightened of many of the things I did not understand and could not control, I did my best to cling to the comfort of family. When that fell short, I would practice a childlike form of magic, hoping that my superstitious rituals would frighten off the various bogeymen and demons that surely lurked just around the corner. And to *really* ensure that the orderly world of today would still be intact tomorrow, I would pray to God. My prayers were simple, taught to me by my Orthodox Jewish grandparents. They (the prayers and my grandparents) affirmed the existence of a single powerful God who was to be praised for the ability to sustain life, protect the children and their loved ones, and delay the inevitable sleep of death.

I delighted in my consciousness of God as it gave me a deep connection not only to the elders in my family but also to the spiritual world beyond the walls of our tight family circle. I learned that the best way to see that world was indirectly, through the lens of the imagination, and during moments of stillness I feasted my mind's eye on its mysteries and wonders.

I created this book for two reasons. The first one was that, as an ambitious adult, I felt that I was losing the ability to intuit a spiritual presence, to visit the special places where God lives. A clue was that suddenly when I looked out my window at the changing seasons, I didn't really see anything at all. My eyes were focused on my work and all the tasks I had to do each day. All the colors and textures of trees and stones, of clouds and vapor trails and stars were gone because I could no longer see them.

Then one morning when I awoke, racing to get to work, I caught a glimpse of the fiery red leaves of a Japanese maple tree in late autumn. For a moment I stopped in my tracks. It was a wake-up call. "There is a world out there," I thought, "and a world beyond that world. And you," I said to myself, "are missing both. If this is what it means to be an adult, you need to find a way to see the world more like a child." And in a flash, I had an image of Snow White, encased in a glass coffin in the forest, guarded by seven childlike men, awaiting the spiritual touch of love to awaken her. I was asleep in my glass house and with no apparent guides, I was very much in need of a spiritual awakening.

It came in the guise of my young children, who at the ages of 5 and 7 began to draw pictures of God.

My daughter, Georgie, created her drawings as a way to search for her identity as a Jewish girl living in a Christian community. In her drawings and through our family discussions, she discovered many sides of God, who loves and protects but who also judges and condemns.

My son's first drawing of God also had to do with our dinner table discussions about religious tolerance and the need to respect all those who see God in their own special ways. But his drawing came from a more specific experience. I had taken him to visit a lovely Christian monastery near our home. As we were walking through a hallway leading to the chapel, we passed a large wooden crucifix hanging low on the wall. Mackey reached up to touch the crucifix and his hand caught on one of the spikes in Christ's feet. When I heard him call my name, I turned around to see a very nervous little boy holding the wooden spike in his hand. I helped him put it back in place and tried to make light of the episode. But I knew that he was shaken and needed to express his feelings. And so Mackey made many drawings of Christ and of Jews and Romans and Christians. And we talked about the God of the Jews and the Christians and the Muslims and the Buddhists and of all the other people in the world.

The second reason for creating this book sprang from these talks and from the drawings. I soon found myself looking for God outside my window and inside my heart. I began asking spiritual questions I thought I had left behind many, many years ago—"What is God? Where is God? How can I be certain that God is present? If God is loving, why do so many people hate and hurt each other because they see God in a different way?"

Because I could not answer the questions myself, I asked several of my colleagues and mentors, and they had answers, but they were poor ones, just empty words. Then Sue Jennings, a dear old friend and colleague with the spirit of a child in her heart, visited from Britain. She had accompanied Mackey and me to the monastery and witnessed Mackey's accidental encounter with Christ's spike and the subsequent drawings of God by Mackey and Georgie. We talked for a long time. She asked me, "Wouldn't it be wonderful if you asked children from all around the world to draw pictures of God and to tell you in their own words how they saw God?" And so, happily accepting a bit of Sue's midwifery, this book was pushed further into being.

I traveled far and wide, sometimes taking my own children along. And because I couldn't travel everywhere, I asked friends and colleagues who lived in faraway places to speak to children and ask them to draw pictures and to tell stories about God. I contacted children of many races and religions, children from wealthy families and children living in poverty, children from countries at war and children from peaceful countries, happy children and sad ones. Children were interviewed in countries as far away as China and Japan and as close as the center of my small Hudson River town. I decided to speak to children between the ages of 3 and 13: the young ones just old enough to express their thoughts in words and pictures, and the older ones just young enough to be close to the wonder of the spiritual world.

Some 500 children participated in this project. They came from more than 30 countries and from more than 20 different spiritual orientations, including Christian and Jewish, Muslim and Hindu, Buddhist and Taoist, Baha'i and native peoples. I discovered that their spiritual images reflected a great deal of their material circumstances, and I tentatively concluded that the children's conceptions of God were determined as much by culture and class as by religious orientation.

Although there are great differences between the spiritual landscapes created by children from East and West, from poverty and from plenty, there are also many commonalities that I hope you will discover as you engage with these images. Generally speaking, I found that all the children had a need to create a personal vision of the divine, a spiritual world that mirrors their culture and inner psychological states. There are many reasons for this need. Perhaps the primary one is to search for explanations of the great mysteries of the world—where we come from and what will become of us in life and death. In creating God through pictures and stories, children provide explanations for themselves in a poetic language of images all their own.

This book is for those of you who wish to revisit the origins of your spiritual consciousness. It is a reminder that there are more ways of seeing and more worlds to be seen than meets the eye. When you look at these pictures and read these words, make sure to put on the right set of lenses, the ones that will lead you to your own images of the spiritual. It could be that the figure in the glass box is not Snow White awaiting her prince, but the beautiful part of us all that lies dormant, waiting for the right moment to be awakened to the wonders of the universe. But first, a story:

> A 10-year-old girl is hard at work in class drawing a picture.
>
> The teacher approaches and asks, "What are you doing?"
>
> The girl replies, "I am drawing God."
>
> "But nobody has ever seen God," says the teacher.
>
> The girl looks up and responds: "You will in a minute."

THE BIRTH—YANNA, 6 YEARS OLD, NONDENOMINATIONAL, SOUTH AFRICA

A Story from South Africa

ONCE UPON A TIME THERE WAS A BABY WITH A HUGE heart inside and nothing else, except blood and God. She was called Yanna and had huge wings. She was flying up to the clouds and singing a song about herself. God was having lunch and taking a break to say hello. Yanna is feeling happy and is looking all over the place because she is new born.

—Yanna, 6 years old, Nondenominational, South Africa

God lives in glass and is shaped by the wind.

—Natasha, 7 years old, Christian, South Africa

God lives above the attic, in the sky.

—Virraj, 6 years old, Hindu, India

God lives on a star. He has no eyes or mouth. He is like a star, himself. There is not such a big star anywhere. I haven't seen him yet. I have been looking for him, for the star.

—Philip, 4 years old, Orthodox Christian, Bulgaria

God is in the world but we don't see him. We feel him in the stomach when he knocks.

—Shakked, 7 years old, Jewish, Israel

God lives in his house with his wife, Maria, and they stay there.

—Konstandia, 6 years old, Greek Orthodox, Greece

God lives in our hearts.

—Erik, 10 years old, Catholic, Gypsy (Romanos), Czech Republic

God lives in a place with clean clouds and fresh air to keep the soul clear.

—Sang Mi, 10 years old, Christian, Korea

God lives in the sky with the clouds. This is God's finger. God is a He. He can talk to people. He's pointing his finger at Rachel from the Bible and saying: "I want the world to be peaceful." Rachel wants to help but she doesn't know how.

—Georgie, 7 years old, Jewish, USA

THE HAND OF GOD—GEORGIE, 7 YEARS OLD, JEWISH, USA

GOD LIVES IN HEAVEN AND IN THE HEART—FREDERIKE, 9 YEARS OLD, CATHOLIC, GERMANY

It's time to celebrate. The angels blow their trumpets. After that, they have tea. A boy is coming to heaven.

—India, 5 years old, Pentecostal
Britain

In Indian religion, God is not in a certain place, like the sky. He is everywhere. God is always in your heart and you have to bring it out if you want to pray to him.

—Shivani, 12 years old, Hindu
USA

God is a feeling. He's a feeling for everything. We don't really know what he is. Other people might believe in something different so he is all things and all religions. God was originally instinct. Instinct is an invisible force telling you what's right and wrong, like the conscience in Pinocchio. He's not just for one religion. He's good and bad, all emotions, everything.

—Andrew, 8 years old, Jewish
USA

I believe in God because when I have problems I pray. After praying, I feel better than before.

—Brian, 8 years old, Confucian
Taiwan

God gives apples to Adam and Eve. If they eat the forbidden one, they become bad.

—Antonella, 8 years old, Catholic
Switzerland

God eayts froots. He eayts food. Yum, yum, it is good.

—Liora, 5 years old, Christian
USA

In heaven, everything's magical. If you wish for an apple, God will give you a whole tree.

—Rizwanul, 11 years old, Muslim
Bangladesh

God's Apples—Antonella, 8 years old, Catholic, Switzerland

PREGNANT GOD—BEN, 9 YEARS OLD, CATHOLIC, USA

God seems to look like a girl.

—José, 7 years old, Catholic
Portugal

God is naked but he's covered up by clouds. God, it's a man's name. He's a man. He has lifted his hands to say hello, hello to God's people, human beings and aliens. I wonder if God ever gets pregnant? Probably not. He beams babies out of his head into his hands and puts them in the mothers on earth.

—Ben, 9 years old, Catholic
USA

God has a belly button. I love him because he gives us money.

—George, 8 years old, Greek Orthodox, Gypsy (Romanos)
Greece

It is not allowed in my religion to draw God. So I draw a chair of gold in the middle of the sky on which he sits. He is seeing but not seen. God can do miracles. I must keep his commandments and laws and study Torah each second so that he will not destroy the world.

—Gil, 9 years old, Jewish
Israel

Allah has no form but he has power.

—Nyla, 9 years old, Muslim
USA

I learned to recognize God because of the top-knot on his head.

—Meher, 9 years old, Sikh
India

God's Golden Chair—Gil, 9 years old, Jewish, Israel

God Has a Long Sword——Chang Mong, 10 years old, Taoist, Taiwan

God lives very high up and no one can find his place. There are many soldiers that protect him. When devils attack, they will be defeated. There is a long sword in his hand. Nobody's blade can hurt him. If I disobey God, God will turn me into a soldier.

—Chang Mong, 10 years old, Taoist
Taiwan

God's enemy is a 70-year-old man who wants to kill God with a rifle but will not succeed because the bullet cannot reach the high sky.

—Karin, 7 years old, Jewish
Israel

The devil goes up and gets people and tells them: "Come with me. I'll show you something." And then he forces them to work for him and to be his slaves. They bring him food and he lies in his bed and he says: "Do this and do that!" And they are exhausted, and they still have to work, because if they can't anymore, they will die. The devil lives in a cave in which everything is red. And then God makes himself black and the devil is scared of black. And then the devil says: "Help! Help!" And then the slaves run away because he doesn't notice. And then the devil has to look for new ones.

—Hannah, 6 years old, Christian
Austria

A Story from the former Yugoslavia

GOD IS LIKE AN OLD LOVING FATHER WHO CLOSELY FOLLOWS all his children, especially the poorest and the weakest. A child named Sinsha lives in a suburb of Sarajevo, destroyed in the war. He shakes with the chill and hasn't eaten in two days. He sadly gazes at his hat, left on the ground to beg for money. He thinks back to a few months before when the war hadn't come yet. He thinks of the smiling faces of his parents and the cheerful shout of his little sister. But the horrible memory of the bomb that destroyed his house and killed his family makes him feel bad. He hears a voice say: "Remember that you are not alone. I will always be there to help you." He knew that voice and said: "Lord, I'm so cold and I haven't eaten in the past two days. Make sure that someone notices me." The voice remained silent but after a few minutes, a patrol of the United Nations passed by and seeing that the boy was pale and numb with cold, gave him food and comfort and took him to a camp for poor children.

—Wanda, 10 years old, Catholic, Italy

GOD AMONG THE POOR—WANDA, 10 YEARS OLD, CATHOLIC, ITALY

THE PROTECTIVE COVER OF GOD—MARTA, 11 YEARS OLD, CATHOLIC, SPAIN

God wants peace to be everywhere and the children should be happy. There was war in Bosnia. They shooted on a tree, you can still see it, and the tree had no leaves. It still has no leaves, no more leaves on the tree. When God defeats all his enemies, the sun will shine and then it will be winter and Santa Claus will pack all the presents and give them to the children.

—Anita, 8 years old, Muslim
Bosnia and Herzegovina

God appears and is sitting in heaven with a stick because he has a back-ache and he doesn't want to fall over. If I could talk to God I'd tell him that some kids pick on me, some grownups, too. They curse me and I say to them why are you cursing me, have I cursed you? I have nothing against you. I will tell him that. God spends his time talking to the bad guys. He tells them: "When Christ was nailed I told him to curse them, but Christ didn't curse them because he was sorry for them."

—Panagiotis, 8 years old, Greek Orthodox, Gypsy (Romanos)
Greece

God protects the good and the bad, black and yellow, red and white. He rejects sorrow, broken hearts, war, injustice and weapons. God has us under a protective shell, like the turtle. This protects us from everything.

—Marta, 11 years old, Catholic
Spain

God has huge ears so he can hear when the children cry and everything that people say.

—Vanessa, 7 years old, Lutheran
Germany

God has black eyes so at night nobody will see him.

—Adam, 7 years old, Catholic
Northern Ireland

God's tummy is red and that means he is very holy.

—Eunan, 5 years old, Catholic
Northern Ireland

On the back of God's head is a box with a key.

—David, 10 years old, Jewish
USA

GOD'S EARS—VANESSA, 7 YEARS OLD, LUTHERAN, GERMANY

Rain Is God's Tears—Mackey, 5 years old, Jewish, USA

God has 4 arms and lives with an invisible dog in a castle in the sky. Rain is God's tears.

—Mackey, 5 years old, Jewish
USA

I think rain is when God is spraying polish on the earth to make it clean. It rains a lot here in Ireland so it should be pretty clean.

—Lauren, 8 years old, Protestant
Northern Ireland

God was in a rush when he made the rain, so I got a little wet.

—Kyōhei, 7 years old, Catholic
Japan

God sends an angel to watch over one person and to protect her til her death and make her go on the right path. Then God calls the child that he wants to go to paradise. He has a big book in his hands and tells her the bad things she did in her life. Then he says that she can enter paradise and there is no more evil. She can be happy. The gate is opened. Everybody is celebrating, the little birds and the butterflies celebrate and there is a big feast the whole day long. Here is the gate that God opens to let the child in.

—Rosaria, 8 years old, Catholic
Switzerland

God comes down from heaven and asks the girl, Elisa, if she wants to go with him to heaven to see the angels, to tell her tales and to see a lot of beautiful things. Elisa answers: "It would be great. I would love to go." God brings her with him. God is kind and brings Elisa back to her house. God brought her to heaven, because Elisa loved him a lot.

—Lavinia, 8 years old, Catholic
Italy

Not everyone goes straight to heaven. You can go to hell or puberty or something.

—Máire, 11 years old, Catholic
Northern Ireland

THE GATE OF PARADISE—ROSARIA, 8 YEARS OLD, CATHOLIC, SWITZERLAND

THE INFINITE SOURCE OF HAPPINESS—KIMON, 10 YEARS OLD, NONDENOMINATIONAL, SOUTH AFRICA

God is an infinite source of happiness and he gives everything he has. He loves everyone. God is strong and beautiful. He caused the big bang that formed the earth and the first humans. I believe in science and God.

—Kimon, 10 years old, Nondenominational
South Africa

God is kind of like...you know Jesus? You know that kind of guy? That's the Christian religion. We're kind of a different religion, but we think of the Christian people. That's one thing you're supposed to do. I think that God is kind of a person that's spiritually real. He thinks of every religion. He could be the valley, the sea, the clouds, the sky, anything. He made up people and trees and flowers. He was the kind of person that made dinosaurs. Nobody knows how they got killed. It's just that he makes new things if they run out.

—Desire, 6 years old, Baha'i
Canada

God hurt his eye. He walked into a wall by accident because he was blind. He was trying to get a taxi and he didn't know that the wall was there. He took a taxi because he wanted to go home to see his child for Christmas. "Child, I'm sorry," said God. "I don't have any money to buy you a present for Christmas." But God gets magic powers from Santa. He uses his magic to give his child a teddy bear.

—Ossycha, 6 years old, Inuit (Nuu-Chal-Nath tribe)
Canada

Once there was a God who created everything in the world and he lived where the dinosaurs were. Something happened to God, he became blind and then joined up with someone who could see so he would not bump into things. And when he bumps into something it goes boom and then it will inflate again. The clouds have always been there, but God is much older than the clouds. And when the dinosaurs did not live anymore, we were in this world.

—Christian, 10 years old, Protestant
Germany

Blind God—Ahmed, 10 years old, Muslim, Turkey/Germany

Isis—Jasmine, 10 years old, First Nations, Canada

When I was five Isis was there waiting for me, and we went into space. And then we walked on the moon. She said: "I love you." That's all I remember.

—Jasmine, 10 years old, First Nations
Canada

I went to the mountains and there lightning struck into the big trees. The trees fell down on me. Suddenly, God appeared in a cave and pushed the trees off me. I was saved. I told him thank you, and I went home.

—Ladislav, 10 years old, Atheist
Czech Republic

God is a tree. The leaves are his sons and the branches are his daughters. All creation is around him. The river is heaven.

—Athena, 9 years old, Protestant
USA

Once upon a time an angel was lost and he arrived at the star of God. He asked God: "Lord, I am lost. What way must I choose?" God said: "The way of love."

—Judith, 10 years old, Catholic
Spain

The girl is Avalokitesvara, the Goddess of Mercy. She protects the earth. Her house is above the clouds. She sits on her throne. When she looks at the alarm clock she knows that it is time to pray. So she leaves the throne and goes to the room to meditate. She chants the Buddhist sutras and fingers the Buddhist beads. Because chanting the sutras has to be silent, she does not move and has to concentrate in her mind. Then she goes back to the throne and sits straight. When it is time for rest, she goes to bed.

—E-Fan, 8 years old, Buddhist
Taiwan

We worship God. We believe in and worship Santoshi Ma and also believe in Shankar. I have seen God in the form of man, and God can also be seen in children. God lives in the sky. God lives in our minds. And I have also seen God in a dream. Sai Baba sits in a peepal tree. We also worship Lord Ganesha. We can do anything for God. God talks to me. A teacher is also a kind of God. We revere our mothers and fathers. That is all I know about God.

—Pooja, 9 years old, Hindu
India

THE GODDESS OF MERCY—E-FAN, 8 YEARS OLD, BUDDHIST, TAIWAN

God's Balloons—Naama, 10 years old, Jewish, Israel

Many years ago lived a man that went to heaven and became God. People sent him balloons with wishes written on them. God tried to fulfill every wish.

—Naama, 10 years old, Jewish
Israel

I imagine God like Jesus, a little old, with long hair. He is dressed in a white tunic with short sleeves and has wings. He lives in heaven, in an all-white sky, with a few clouds here and there. At the center there is a big arm chair, all embroidered, where God sits. Everyone that dies and goes to Heaven has his little cloud. God asks them how they are doing in Heaven and if they want to see someone that died before. Every cloud can be opened, just like a jewel case and inside there are a lot of things that can be taken out, just like from Mary Poppins' bag.

—Francesca, 10 years old, Catholic
Italy

My grandpa died and became God. His jewelry and his clothes are golden and the sky is everywhere around him.

—Ester, 5 years old, Jewish
Bulgaria

God lives seven skies high. God judges who is bad and who is good. The bad people go to the devil. The good people go to heaven. When you die, God takes the soul. He keeps them. They are invisible and at night they visit the family. Angels are people who die. God makes angels. We pray to God to be a good person and make our family healthy and make sick people well and have money.

—Mohammad, 11 years old, Muslim
Bangladesh

One day a boy had a dream about an adult on a cloud which he thought might be Jesus. And there were people that already had died and gone up to heaven and there were angels with trumpets and the kid had a vision that he would go up there one day. And after the dream, he repented and felt like he was forgiven.

—Kurtis, 9 years old, Mormon
Canada

SEVEN SKIES HIGH—MOHAMMAD, 11 YEARS OLD, MUSLIM, BANGLADESH

THE TEN HANDS OF DURGA
—MONDIRA, 10 YEARS OLD, HINDU, INDIA

GOD'S SON GANESH AND A MOUSE
—SHREYA, 11 YEARS OLD, HINDU, INDIA

Three Stories from India

ONE DAY, GOD TOLD HIS WIFE TO TRAVEL INTO TIME. His wife left on a big white bird. She had lots of fun and found a magic forest full of beautiful flowers, animals and trees. She dug a tunnel and made friends with a snake who lived nearby. They called God over. He came at night, riding on the moon. They all danced and ate and drank. When they felt tired, they all went to sleep under a big tree.

—Mondira, 10 years old, Hindu, India

When Narayan came to God he told him all about the people of the world and about all the bad things. Then Shivji got very angry and he did the Dance of Death, Tandar Nritya. When this happens, all the bad ends. There is one god in ourselves but there is also an evil in ourselves. We have to fight our evil.

—Anamika, 10 years old, Hindu, India

One day the mother of the god Kartik asked him to go around the world. So he encircled her three times and sat down. She asked him why he did not do as he was told. He said he'd gone around her thrice. She was the world.

—Shreya, 11 years old, Hindu, India

God is deep blue. He gives me good ideas.

—Luke, 5 years old, Christian
Britain

God is half human being, half something else I can't describe. God will age without a wrinkled face and is immortal. God lives at the end of the sky but the children do not know where he is. There are beautiful clouds below God and a castle above God. The child and the bird in the picture have died and stay in rooms of this castle. You can always meet God when you arrive for the first time in the sky or when you want to ask God for a favor. I can't color him because God doesn't have any of the colors of this world.

—Yeha, 6 years old, Confucian
Korea

White and yellow are the colors of heaven. They are clean and bright. God waits at a desk with a big book with everybody's names and an angel checks the book and gives out the halos.

—Nadja, 10 years old, Catholic
Northern Ireland/Iraq

The sky in heaven has lots of colors and everyone is asleep except God.

—Kristy, 4 years old, Pentecostal
Britain

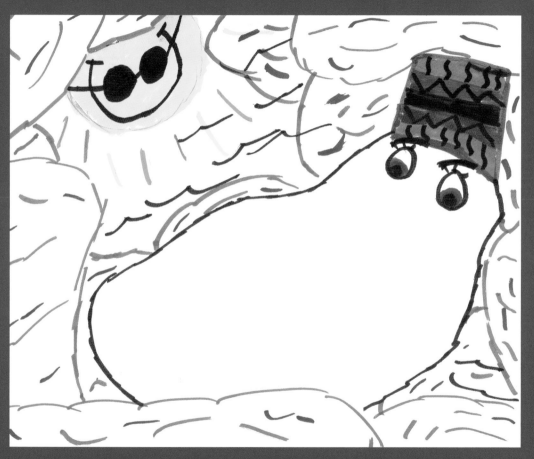

THE COLOR OF GOD—MINA, 9 YEARS OLD, BAHA'I, CANADA/IRAN

The Gates to heaven. Everyone is aloud in.

GOD IS A LIGHT—ODI, 10 YEARS OLD, CATHOLIC, NIGERIA/BRITAIN

God is a light. He is shining love on the whole of earth. The lines coming down from God's eyes are love.

—Odi, 10 years old, Catholic
Nigeria/Britain

God is a ray of light that shows us the good way.

—Lihi, 10 years old, Jewish
Israel

One day a large mass of kindness, love and light by the name of God saw the empty, dark world spinning in its orbit with not a spot of light. "How much the world needs sunshine to brighten up its sky." So he took his light and made the sun so it wasn't dark anymore.

—Francesca, 13 years old, Baha'i
USA

No one can see the real God. But I see really, really bright lights.

—Sahar, 8 years old, Muslim
Pakistan

In the middle of God's body there is a heart. The red light says pray. When people want to pray really hard, he sends the red light to help. The orange light says love. The yellow light says help.

—Gloria, 10 years old, Catholic
Uganda/Britain

I have drawn this picture representing God. I have labeled him. The pink bits are the skin. The red bits are the muscle. The yellow is God's love and the Holy Spirit. I think you can see God through people just by looking at them, just by listening to them, getting to know their personality. I believe God is in all of us.

—Joshua, 9 years old, Catholic
Dominican Republic/Britain

I cannot draw God because he cannot be seen. The best way to see God is to let the paper be clear, empty. Although we cannot see God, he is around us, in the earth and in heaven at the same time.

—Tomás, 10 years old, Catholic
Czech Republic

GOD IS IN ALL OF US—JOSHUA, 9 YEARS OLD, CATHOLIC, DOMINICAN REPUBLIC/BRITAIN

God Is a Horse-Man—Plamen, 9 years old, Eastern Orthodox, Bulgaria

God is good but revengeful. His punishment is death or a bad disease. God doesn't die. He has a tail. His hair is like horse's. He's holding a trident. He uses it to make thunders. When he's angry, he makes storms, like last night's one. Wow! He got angry at someone, probably a priest who did something wrong in the church. I pray in the church. Sometimes I confess my sins but not to the priest, just to myself. If God doesn't forgive me, I could get sick and die. But I'm not afraid of him.

—Plamen, 9 years old, Eastern Orthodox
Bulgaria

People shot God and the fire became coal. Nobody believes in God. In kindergarten they told us stories about how God created the sea and the sun. When I talked to God in kindergarten, he didn't answer me. I was mad at God.

—Erez, 6 years old, Jewish
Israel

Satan is dancing and God prefers those who pray to those who sing and dance.

—Musta, 11 years old, Muslim
Israel

This is God's chair and he's looking down at all the people and he's watching us. And he's making sure that if anything bad happens, that he can try and fix it. I don't think he can really talk but somehow you can kind of feel what he's saying. He's wearing a hat that has carpet material around it. It's his favorite hat and the only thing he wears. God has created everything. If there was no God, there would just be nothing.

—Mina, 9 years old, Baha'i
Canada/Iran

Heavenly Father and Jesus split the earth and put all the people who believe in them in it and close it up. After the earthquake, they open it up and make a whole new generation.

—Lauren, 9 years old, Mormon
Canada

When everyone dies and there is no one else in the world, God is going to move all the graveyards and bring all the dinosaurs back.

—Cory, 6 years old, Nondenominational
USA

JESUS' MESSAGE TO US—RYAN, 10 YEARS OLD, CHRISTIAN, USA

This is Tathagata, the one who will grow up to be Buddha. All is peaceful around Tathagata. There are no enemies, no bad things. Everything is calm.

—Pei-Zo, 8 years old, Taoist
Taiwan

I have seen Lord Shiva in a dream and I dreamt that when I got entangled then Shiva was able to free me from the tangle.

—Sonu, 10 years old, Hindu
India

I saw God on television. He was a fat man with a very nice and deep voice. God is very old, about 102. There is a soul of a dead person in my picture. It is flying up to God.

—Sandra, 10 years old, Lutheran
Germany

God sits in a stone.

—Sirajul, 6 years old, Muslim
Bangladesh

When less than 100 people stop believing in God, he dies.

—Michael, 8 years old, Jewish
USA

THE YOUNG BUDDHA—PEI-ZO, 8 YEARS OLD, TAOIST, TAIWAN

Magician God Who Rides the Clouds—Sang Min, 8 years old, Christian, Korea

A Story from Israel

ONCE UPON A TIME WHEN GOD WENT OUT FOR A WALK IN THE sky to scatter all the stars, he noticed that one star in his bag was crying. When he asked it why, the star said: "I am crying because I am old and soon someone will take my place. I can see him below—a man who has just died. Now he will take my place." "Don't worry, dear star," said God. "I will change this." And God went down to earth and he found the dead man and he said: "You will become a new star. You will not take the place of any star in the sky." And he lifted the man's soul from his body and brought the new star to the heavens and he smiled. The old star started to laugh and rejoice and dance. Then God drew out the new star from his bag and the sky turned violet and the sun set and the moon rose. Angels appeared and served cake and wine in ivory glasses and there was a great party in the sky. Then God said: "Here I crown the new star, one of our beautiful souls that are now in the sky." And so it was. From that day on to the end of the years, there is the old star that wept and asked not to be replaced and the new star, the young and beautiful, that has come and joined the world of stars.

—Galia, 8 years old, Jewish, Israel

Your heart is for love and goodness. The heart is in heaven, but heaven kicked the heart out. Jehovah didn't like that. He gets mad and kicks the heaven out. Then he puts the heart back in heaven. Hearts eat cookies.

—Christopher, 5 years old, Jehovah's Witness
USA

God is in my heart, peeping out and saying hello.

—Yanna, 6 years old, Nondenominational
South Africa

God does not need jewels. He has them in his heart.

—Mondira, 10 years old, Hindu
India

God has a very big heart, but he is missing a little part. My heart is full. I give that missing part to him.

—Andrea, 8 years old, Catholic
Mexico

God lives in the soul. He wants people to love and respect each other and take care of all the living things. They all can feel. They all are alive.

—Joanna, 11 years old, Eastern Orthodox
Bulgaria

God is like children because children are little and God is big.

—Jenny, 5 years old, Buddhist
China/USA

GOD THE COMFORTER—BIANCA, 12 YEARS OLD, LUTHERAN, GERMANY

An Afterword

Before you put down this book, I offer a final story, one I have heard in three different countries.

> A four-year-old boy asks his parents if he can speak to his new baby
>
> sister alone. The sister is just two weeks old. The parents, though a bit
>
> skeptical, finally agree and listen in at the door. "Can you tell me what
>
> God looks like?" says the boy to the infant. "I'm starting to forget."

We may never know empirically what God looks like or where God lives. But if we keep looking for God's many shapes through the lens of our childlike consciousness, we will surely remember what it is like to awaken to all the wonders of the universe.

Pause now and then in your busy day and look out the glass to the sky and beyond and see with your heart.

About SKYLIGHT PATHS Publishing

SkyLight Paths Publishing is creating a place where people of different spiritual traditions come together for challenge and inspiration, a place where we can help each other understand the mystery that lies at the heart of our existence.

Through spirituality, our religious beliefs are increasingly becoming a part of our lives—rather than *apart* from our lives. While many of us may be more interested than ever in spiritual growth, we may be less firmly planted in traditional religion. Yet, we do want to deepen our relationship to the sacred, to learn from our own as well as from other faith traditions, and to practice in new ways.

SkyLight Paths sees both believers and seekers as a community that increasingly transcends traditional boundaries of religion and denomination—people wanting to learn from each other, *walking together, finding the way.*

We at SkyLight Paths take great care to produce beautiful books that present meaningful spiritual content in a form that reflects the art of making high quality books. Therefore, we want to acknowledge those who contributed to the production of this book.

PRODUCTION
Tim Holtz, Bridgett Taylor & Marian B. Wallace

EDITORIAL
Amanda Dupuis, Sandra Korinchak, Martha McKinney,
Polly Short & Emily Wichland

JACKET DESIGN
Drena Fagen, New York, New York

TEXT DESIGN
Bronwen Battaglia, Scituate, Massachusetts

Other Interesting Books—Spirituality

Who Is My God? *An Innovative Guide to Finding Your Spiritual Identity*
Created by *the Editors at SkyLight Paths*

Spiritual Type™ + Tradition Indicator = Spiritual Identity

Your Spiritual Identity is an undeniable part of who you are—whether you've thought much about it or not. This dynamic resource provides a helpful framework to begin or deepen spiritual growth. Includes the unique Spiritual Identity Self-Test™. "An innovative and entertaining way to think—and rethink—about your own spiritual path, or perhaps even to find one." —Dan Wakefield, author of *How Do We Know When It's God?* 6 x 9, 160 pp, Quality PB Original, ISBN 1-893361-08-X **$15.95**

Praying with Our Hands: *Twenty-One Practices of Embodied Prayer from the World's Spiritual Traditions*
by *Jon M. Sweeney*; Photographs by *Jennifer J. Wilson*;
Foreword by *Mother Tessa Bielecki*; Afterword by *Taitetsu Unno, Ph.D.*

A spiritual guidebook for bringing prayer into our bodies.

This inspiring book of reflections and accompanying photographs shows twenty-one simple ways of using our hands to speak to God. Spiritual traditions represented include Anglican, Sufi, Zen, Roman Catholic, Yoga, Shaker, Hindu, Jewish, Pentecostal, Eastern Orthodox, and many others.
8 x 8, 96 pp, 22 duotone photographs, Quality PB Original, ISBN 1-893361-16-0 **$16.95**

How to Be a Perfect Stranger, In 2 Volumes: *A Guide to Etiquette in Other People's Religious Ceremonies*
Ed. by *Stuart M. Matlins* & *Arthur J. Magida* AWARD WINNERS!

Explains the rituals and celebrations of North America's major religions/denominations, helping an interested guest to feel comfortable, participate to the fullest extent possible, and avoid violating anyone's religious principles. Answers practical questions from the perspective of *any* other faith.

Vol. 1: North America's Largest Faiths Assemblies of God • Baptist • Buddhist • Christian Science • Episcopalian/Anglican • Greek Orthodox • Hindu • Islam • Jewish • Lutheran • Methodist • Mormon • Presbyterian • Quaker • Roman Catholic • Seventh-day Adventist • United Church of Christ • many others 6 x 9, 432 pp, Quality PB, ISBN 1-893361-01-2 **$19.95**

Vol. 2: More Faiths in North America African American Methodist Churches • Baha'i • Church of the Brethren • Evangelical Free Church • Mennonite/Amish • Native American/First Nations • Orthodox Churches • Pentecostal Church of God • Reformed Church • Sikh • Unitarian Universalist • Wesleyan • many others 6 x 9, 416 pp, Quality PB, ISBN 1-893361-02-0 **$19.95**

Or phone, fax, mail or e-mail to: SKYLIGHT PATHS Publishing
Sunset Farm Offices, Route 4 • P.O. Box 237 • Woodstock, Vermont 05091
Tel: (802) 457-4000 • Fax: (802) 457-4004 • www.skylightpaths.com
Credit card orders: (800) 962-4544 (9AM–5PM ET Monday–Friday)
Generous discounts on quantity orders. Satisfaction guaranteed. Prices subject to change.